Johnny Depp

ABDO
Publishing Company

A Big Buddy Book
by **Sarah Tieck**

VISIT US AT
www.abdopublishing.com

Published by ABDO Publishing Company, 8000 West 78th Street, Edina, Minnesota 55439.

Printed in the United States.

Coordinating Series Editor: Rochelle Baltzer
Contributing Editors: Megan M. Gunderson, BreAnn Rumsch, Marcia Zappa
Graphic Design: Maria Hosley
Cover Photograph: *AP Photo*: Matt Sayles
Interior Photographs/Illustrations: *AP Photo*: AP Photo (p. 29), Kristie Bull/graylock.com (p. 20), Joe Cavaretta (p. 7), Kevork Djansezian (p. 25), Paul Drinkwater/NBCU Photo Bank via AP Images (p. 14), HFPA (p. 29), Shizuo Kambayashi (p. 4), Robert E. Klein (p. 20), Remy de la Mauviniere (p. 27), John D. McHugh (p. 22), Danny Moloshok (pp. 5, 23), Chris Pizzello (p. 19), Amy Sancetta (p. 17), Reed Saxon (p. 10), Matt Sayles (p. 27); *Getty Images*: Chris Gordon (p. 9), Barry King/WireImage (pp. 7, 15), Orion Pictures (p. 13); *Photos.com* (16).

Library of Congress Cataloging-in-Publication Data

Tieck, Sarah, 1976-
  Johnny Depp : famous actor / Sarah Tieck.
    p. cm. -- (Big buddy biographies)
  ISBN 978-1-60453-707-9
  1. Depp, Johnny--Juvenile literature. 2. Motion picture actors and actresses--United States--Biography--Juvenile literature. I. Title.

PN2287.D39T58 2009
791.4302'8'092--dc22
  [B]
                          2009000409

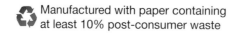

Manufactured with paper containing at least 10% post-consumer waste

Contents

Movie Star

Johnny Depp is a famous actor. He has appeared in television shows and movies. He starred in *Charlie and the Chocolate Factory* and the *Pirates of the Caribbean* movies.

Johnny has won awards for his work. He has been **interviewed** on television shows. And, he has been featured on magazine covers.

Johnny is known to sign autographs for fans.

Johnny has played both funny and serious roles.

5

Family Ties

John Christopher "Johnny" Depp II was born in Owensboro, Kentucky, on June 9, 1963. His parents are Betty Sue Palmer and John Christopher Depp Sr.

Johnny's older brother is Danny. His older sisters are Christie and Debbie.

Where in the World?

Indiana

Ohio

Illinois

West Virginia

Missouri

• Owensboro

Kentucky

Virginia

Tennessee

Betty Sue worked as a waitress. John Sr. helped plan and build cities as a civil engineer.

Tennessee

North Carolina

South Carolina

Alabama

Georgia

ATLANTIC OCEAN

Florida

GULF OF MEXICO

Miramar

Growing Up

In Owensboro, Johnny spent much time with his grandfather, Pawpaw. Pawpaw died when Johnny was just seven.

Around that time, the Depps left Kentucky. They moved to Miramar, Florida. Over the years, they had many different homes in the area.

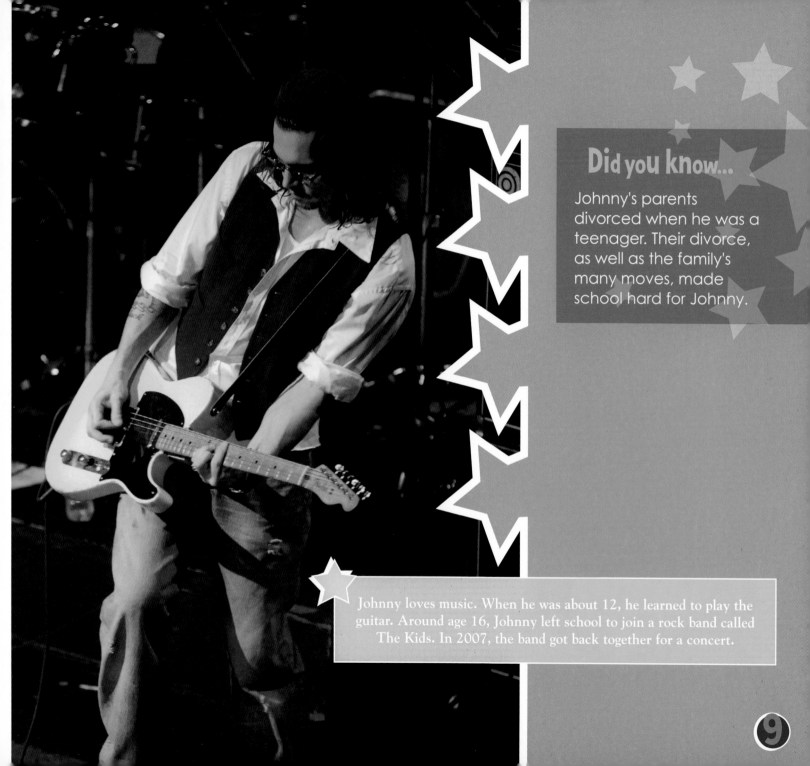

Did you know...

Johnny's parents divorced when he was a teenager. Their divorce, as well as the family's many moves, made school hard for Johnny.

Johnny loves music. When he was about 12, he learned to play the guitar. Around age 16, Johnny left school to join a rock band called The Kids. In 2007, the band got back together for a concert.

Nicholas Cage is an Academy Award–winning actor. He has starred in many films, including the *National Treasure* movies.

Starting Out

When Johnny was 20, he married Lori Anne Allison. Lori introduced Johnny to actor Nicholas Cage. Nicholas helped Johnny get his start in acting. Lori and Johnny divorced after two years.

Early Years

Johnny became a **professional** actor in 1984. His first **role** was in a scary movie called *A Nightmare on Elm Street*.

In 1986, he played a soldier in *Platoon*. This movie was an important step for Johnny. This thoughtful role helped him become a stronger actor. Also, he realized he loved acting.

In *Platoon*, Johnny worked with actors Willem Dafoe, Charlie Sheen, and Tom Berenger (*left to right*). The movie won many awards, including four Oscars!

In 1987, Johnny had his first big television **role**. He played a police officer on *21 Jump Street*. The show was very popular. People soon noticed Johnny's talent.

After about three years, Johnny left the show. Instead, he wanted to play **unique** movie characters. In 1990, he starred in *Edward Scissorhands*. Johnny played a man who has scissors for hands. In the movie, he struggles to fit in and find a family.

Johnny worked with famous director Tim Burton on *Edward Scissorhands*. Tim's films are known for having strange characters.

Off the Screen

Johnny is a father. In 1998, he began dating French actress and singer Vanessa Paradis. They live in southern France with their children. Their daughter Lily-Rose was born in 1999. In 2002, their son Jack was born.

In his free time, Johnny likes to be with his family. Sometimes, they travel to visit Johnny on movie **sets**.

Johnny and his family live near the French Riviera. This area is located on the Mediterranean Sea and is known for its beauty. Many people vacation there.

Johnny says Vanessa is a very important part of his life.

Jack's full name is John Christopher Depp III. He is named for his father and grandfather.

A Pirate's Life

In 2003, Johnny starred in *Pirates of the Caribbean:
The Curse of the Black Pearl*. He played a pirate named
Captain Jack Sparrow.

This movie was very popular. Johnny received awards
for his **role**. He even got his first Oscar **nomination**!

Johnny worked with actors Orlando Bloom and Keira Knightley on the *Pirates of the Caribbean* movies.

19

Johnny got ideas for how to play Captain Jack from Keith Richards. Keith plays guitar with the rock band the Rolling Stones. Johnny says Captain Jack has a rock-and-roll style.

20

Captain Jack became so popular that wax statues have been made of him!

Johnny starred as Captain Jack in two more movies. In 2006, he was in *Pirates of the Caribbean: Dead Man's Chest*. The next year, he was in *Pirates of the Caribbean: At World's End*. In 2008, Johnny won a Nickelodeon Kids' Choice Award for playing Captain Jack.

Johnny isn't finished with the **role** of Captain Jack. In 2009, a fourth *Pirates of the Caribbean* movie was in the works.

Kate Winslet starred with Johnny in *Finding Neverland*. Johnny received another Oscar nomination for his role in the movie.

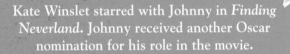

Talented Actor

Johnny has worked on many different movies. In 2004, he acted in *Finding Neverland*. Then in 2005, he starred as Willy Wonka in *Charlie and the Chocolate Factory*. Because he plays such different roles, Johnny is considered very talented!

Many fans were excited about *Charlie and the Chocolate Factory*. It is based on a famous book by Roald Dahl. And, it is a remake of a popular 1971 film.

In 2007, Johnny starred in the **musical** *Sweeney Todd*. Tim Burton directed this film, as well as *Charlie and the Chocolate Factory*. Both movies had interesting **costumes** and **sets**. Johnny wore heavy makeup for these **unique** movies.

Johnny earned another Oscar **nomination** for *Sweeney Todd*. And, he won a Golden Globe Award for his work! Golden Globes honor the year's best movies and television shows.

Sweeney Todd was the sixth film Johnny and Tim have worked on together. Next, they filmed *Alice in Wonderland*. Johnny played the Mad Hatter.

Body Art

Johnny has many tattoos. Pictures and words appear on his arms, hands, legs, and chest.

Each tattoo represents a special story from Johnny's life. He has at least 12 tattoos. And, he continues to add new ones!

Johnny wears special jewelry. His daughter, Lily-Rose, made some of his bracelets.

Johnny has tattoos that say Jack (*left*) and Lily-Rose. He also has a tattoo with his mother's name (*right*).

Johnny enjoys the challenge of playing unusual characters. He wants to continue growing as an actor.

Buzz

Johnny has a bright **future**! He acted in several movies in 2009. He also plans to play Tonto in *The Lone Ranger*, a movie about the Wild West. Fans are excited to see what's next for Johnny Depp!

The Lone Ranger was a famous radio and television show from the 1930s through the 1950s. It was about a masked Texas ranger, his horse Silver, and his sidekick Tonto.

29

Snapshot

⭐**Name**: John Christopher "Johnny" Depp II

⭐**Birthday**: June 9, 1963

⭐**Birthplace**: Owensboro, Kentucky

⭐**Appearances**: *A Nightmare on Elm Street, Platoon, 21 Jump Street, Edward Scissorhands, Donnie Brasco, Pirates of the Caribbean movies, Finding Neverland, Charlie and the Chocolate Factory, Sweeney Todd*

Important Words

costume clothing worn to help show a certain time period, person, place, or thing.

future (FYOO-chuhr) a time that has not yet occurred.

interview to ask someone a series of questions.

musical a story told with music.

nomination the state of being named as a possible winner.

professional (pruh-FEHSH-nuhl) working for money rather than for pleasure.

role a part an actor plays in a show.

set the place where a movie or a television show is recorded.

unique (yu-NEEK) like nothing else.

Web Sites

To learn more about Johnny Depp, visit ABDO Publishing Company online. Web sites about Johnny Depp are featured on our Book Links page. These links are routinely monitored and updated to provide the most current information available.

www.abdopublishing.com

Index